AF110476

OF A HAPPY LIFE

— DE VITA BEATA —

SENECA

« The highest good is a mind which despises the accidents of fortune, and takes pleasure in virtue »

PREFACE

I can say little by way of preface to Seneca's "Minor Dialogs" which I have not already expressed in my preface to *De Benficiis*, except that the "Minor Dialogs" seem to me to be composed in a gloomier key than either *De Beneficiis* or *De Clementia* and probably were written at a time when the author had already begun to experience the ingratitude of his imperial pupil. Some of the dialogs are dated from Corsica, Seneca's place of exile, which he seems to have found peculiarly uncomfortable, although he remarks that there are people who live there from choice. Nevertheless, mournful as they are in tone, these Dialogs have a certain value, because they teach us what was meant by Stoic philosophy in the time of the Twelve Caesars.

I have only to add that the value of my work has been materially enhanced by the kindness of the Rev. Professor

J.E.B. Mayor, who has been good enough to read and correct almost all the proof sheets of this volume.

Aubrey Stewart
London, 1889

CHAPTER ONE

All men, brother Gallio, wish to live happily, but are dull at perceiving exactly what it is that makes life happy: and so far is it from being easy to attain the happiness that the more eagerly a man struggles to reach it the further he departs from it, if he takes the wrong road; for, since this leads in the opposite direction, his very swiftness carries him all the further away. We must therefore first define clearly what it is at which we aim: next we must consider by what path we may most speedily reach it, for on our journey itself, provided it be made in the right direction, we shall learn how much progress we have made each day, and how much nearer we are to the goal towards which our natural desires urge us. But as long as we wander at random, not following any guide except the shouts and discordant clamours of those who invite us to proceed in different directions, our short life will be wasted in useless roamings, even if we labour both day and night to get a good understanding. Let us not therefore decide whither we must tend, and by what path, without the advice of some experienced person who has explored the region which we are about to enter, because this journey is not subject to the same conditions as others; for in them some distinctly understood track and inquiries made of the natives make it impossible for us to go wrong, but here the most beaten and frequented tracks are those which lead us most astray. Nothing, therefore, is more important than that we should not, like sheep, follow the flock that has gone before us, and thus proceed not whither we ought, but whither the rest are going. Now nothing gets us into greater troubles than our subservience to common rumour, and our habit of thinking that those things are best which are most generally received as such, of taking many counterfeits for truly good things, and of living not by reason but by imitation of others. This is the cause of those great heaps into which men rush till they are piled one upon another. In a great crush of people, when the crowd presses upon itself, no one can fall without drawing some one else down upon him, and those who go before cause the destruction of those who follow them. You may observe the same thing in human life: no one can merely go wrong by himself, but he must become both the cause and adviser of another's wrong doing. It is harmful to follow the march of those who go before us, and since every one had rather believe another than form his own opinion, we never pass a deliberate judgment upon life, but some traditional error always entangles us and brings us to ruin, and we perish because we follow other men's examples: we should be cured of this if we were to disengage ourselves from the herd; but as it is, the mob is ready to fight against reason in defence of its own mistake. Consequently the same thing happens as at elections, where, when the fickle breeze of popular favour has veered round, those who have been chosen consuls and praetors are viewed with admiration by the very men who made them so. That we should all approve and disapprove of the same things is the end of every decision which is given according to the voice of the majority.

CHAPTER TWO

When we are considering a happy life, you cannot answer me as though after a division of the House, "This view has most supporters;" because for that very reason it is the worse of the two: matters do not stand so well with mankind that the majority should prefer the better course: the more people do a thing the worse it is likely to be. Let us therefore inquire, not what is most commonly done, but what is best for us to do, and what will establish us in the possession of undying happiness, not what is approved of by the vulgar, the worst possible exponents of truth. By "the vulgar" I mean both those who wear woollen cloaks and those who wear crowns[1]; for I do not regard the colour of the clothes with which they are covered: I do not trust my eyes to tell me what a man is: I have a better and more trustworthy light by which I can distinguish what is true from what is false: let the mind find out what is good for the mind. If a man ever allows his mind some breathing space and has leisure for communing with himself, what truths he will confess to himself, after having been put to the torture by his own self! He will say, "Whatever I have hitherto done I wish were undone: when I think over what I have said, I envy dumb people: whatever I have longed for seems to have been what my enemies would pray might befall me: good heaven, how far more endurable what I have feared seems to be than what I have lusted after. I have been at enmity with many men, and have changed my dislike of them into friendship, if friendship can exist between bad men: yet I have not yet become reconciled to myself," I have striven with all my strength to raise myself above the common herd, and to make myself remarkable for some talent: what have I effected save to make myself a mark for the arrows of my enemies, and show those who hate me where to wound me? Do you see those who praise your eloquence, who covet your wealth, who court your favour, or who vaunt your power? All these either are, or, which comes to the same thing, may be your enemies: the number of those who envy you is as great as that of those who admire you; why do I not rather seek for some good thing which I can use and feel, not one which I can show? these good things which men gaze at in wonder, which they crowd to see, which one points out to another with speechless admiration, are outwardly brilliant, but within are miseries to those who possess them."

1. Lipsius's conjecture, "those who are dressed in white as well as those who are dressed in coloured clothes," alluding to the white robes of candidates for office, seems reasonable.

CHAPTER THREE

Let us seek for some blessing, which does not merely look fine, but is sound and good throughout alike, and most beautiful in the parts which are least seen: let us unearth this. It is not far distant from us; it can be discovered: all that is necessary is to know whither to stretch out your hand: but, as it is, we behave as though we were in the dark, and reach out beyond what is nearest to us, striking as we do so against the very things that we want. However, that I may not draw you into digressions, I will pass over the opinions of other philosophers, because it would take a long time to state and confute them all: take ours. When, however, I say "ours," I do not bind myself to any one of the chiefs of the Stoic school, for I too have a right to form my own opinion. I shall, therefore, follow the authority of some of them, but shall ask some others to discriminate their meaning[1]: perhaps, when after having reported all their opinions, I am asked for my own, I shall impugn none of my predecessors' decisions, and shall say, "I will also add somewhat to them." Meanwhile I follow nature, which is a point upon which every one of the Stoic philosophers are agreed: true wisdom consists in not departing from nature and in moulding our conduct according to her laws and model. A happy life, therefore, is one which is in accordance with its own. nature, and cannot be brought about unless in the first place the mind be sound and remain so without interruption, and next, be bold and vigorous, enduring all things with most admirable courage, suited to the times in which it lives, careful of the body and its appurtenances, yet not troublesomely careful. It must also set due value upon all the things which adorn our lives, without over-estimating any one of them, and must be able to enjoy the bounty of Fortune without becoming her slave. You understand without my mentioning it that an unbroken calm and freedom ensue, when we have driven away all those things which either excite us or alarm us: for in the place of sensual pleasures and and [sic] those slight perishable matters which are connected with the basest crimes, we thus gain an immense, unchangeable, equable joy, together with peace, calmness and greatness of mind, and kindliness: for all savageness is a sign of weakness.

---

1. The Latin words are literally "to divide" their vote, that is, "to separate things of different kinds comprised in a single vote so that they might be voted for separately." — Andrews.

   Sénèque fait allusion ici à une coutume pratiquée dans les assemblés du Sénat; et il nous explique lui-même ailleurs d'un manière très claire:

"Si quelqu'un dans le Sénat," dit-il, "ouvre un avis, dont une partie me convienne, je le somme de la détacher du reste, et j'y adhère." - Ep. 21 - La Grange. [Translated: Here Seneca refers to a custom practiced in the Senate assemblies; and he explains himself to us elsewhere very clearly: "If someone in the Senate," he says, "begins an opinion, of which part suits me, I order him to detach it from the rest, and I subscribe to it." *Letter 21* - La Grange.]

CHAPTER FOUR

Our highest good may also be defined otherwise that is to say, the same idea may be expressed in different language. Just as the same army may at one time be extended more widely, at another contracted into a smaller compass, and may either be curved towards the wings by a depression in the line of the centre, or drawn up in a straight line, while, in whatever figure it be arrayed, its strength and loyalty remain unchanged; so also our definition of the highest good may in some cases be expressed diffusely and at great length, while in others it is put into a short and concise form. Thus, it will come to the same thing, if I say "The highest good is a mind which despises the accidents of fortune, and takes pleasure in virtue": or, "It is an unconquerable strength of mind, knowing the world well, gentle in its dealings, showing great courtesy and consideration for those with whom it is brought into contact." Or we may choose to define it by calling that man happy who knows good and bad only in the form of good or bad minds: who worships honour, and is satisfied with his own virtue, who is neither puffed up by good fortune nor cast down by evil fortune, who knows no other good than that which he is able to bestow upon himself, whose real[?] pleasure lies in despising pleasures. If you choose to pursue this digression further, you can put this same idea into many other forms, without impairing or weakening its meaning: for what prevents our saying that a happy life consists in a mind which is free, upright, undaunted, and steadfast, beyond the influence of fear or desire, which thinks nothing good except honour, and nothing bad except blame[?], and regards everything else as a mass of mean details which can neither add anything to nor take anything away from the happiness of life, but which come and go without either increasing or diminishing the highest good? A man of these principles, whether he will or no, must be accompanied by a continual cheerfulness, a high happiness, which comes indeed from on high because he delights in what he has, and desires no greater pleasures than those which his home affords. Is he not right in allowing these to turn the scale against petty, ridiculous and shortlived movements of his wretched body? on the day on which he becomes proof against pleasure he also becomes proof against pain. See, on the other hand, how evil and guilty a slavery the man is forced to serve who is dominated in turn by pleasures and pains, those most untrustworthy and passionate of masters. We must, therefore, escape from them into freedom. This nothing will bestow upon us save contempt of Fortune: but if we attain to this, then there will dawn upon us those invaluable blessings, the repose of a mind that is at rest in a safe haven, its lofty imaginings, its great and steady delight at casting out errors and learning to know the truth, its courtesy, and its cheerfulness, in all of which we shall take delight, not regarding them as good things, but as proceeding from the proper good of man.

CHAPTER FIVE

Since I have begun to make my definitions without a too strict adherence to the letter, a man may be called "happy" who, thanks to reason, has ceased either to hope or to fear: but rocks also feel neither fear nor sadness, nor do cattle, yet no one would call those things happy which cannot comprehend what happiness is. With them you may class men whose dull nature and want of self-knowledge reduces them to the level of cattle, mere animals: there is no difference between the one and the other, because the latter have no reason, while the former have only a corrupted form of it, crooked and cunning to their own hurt. For no one can be styled happy who is beyond the influence of truth: and consequently a happy life is unchangeable, and is founded upon a true and trustworthy discernment; for the mind is uncontaminated and freed from all evils only when it is able to escape not merely from wounds but also from scratches, when it will always be able to maintain the position which it has taken up, and defend it even against the angry assaults of Fortune: for with regard to sensual pleasures, though they were to surround one on every side, and use every means of assault, trying to win over the mind by caresses and making trial of every conceivable stratagem to attract either our entire selves or our separate parts, yet what mortal that retains any traces of human origin would wish to be tickled day and night, and, neglecting his mind, to devote himself to bodily enjoyments?

CHAPTER SIX

"But," says our adversary, "the mind also will have pleasures of its own." Let it have them, then, and let it sit in judgment over luxury and pleasures; let it indulge itself to the full in all those matters which give sensual delights: then let it look back upon what it enjoyed before, and with all those faded sensualities fresh in its memory let it rejoice and look eagerly forward to those other pleasures which it experienced long ago, and intends to experience again, and while the body lies in helpless repletion in the present, let it send its thoughts onward towards the future, and take stock of its hopes: all this will make it appear, in my opinion, yet more wretched, because it is insanity to choose evil instead of good: now no insane person can be happy, and no one can be sane if he regards what is injurious as the highest good and strives to obtain it. The happy man, therefore, is he who can make a right judgment in all things: he is happy who in his present circumstances, whatever they may be, is satisfied and on friendly terms with the conditions of his life. That man is happy, whose reason recommends to him the whole posture of his affairs.

CHAPTER SEVEN

Even those very people who declare the highest good to be in the belly, see what a dishonourable position they have assigned to it: and therefore they say that pleasure cannot be parted from virtue, and that no one can either live honourably without living cheerfully, nor yet live cheerfully without living honourably. I do not see how these very different matters can have any connexion with one another. What is there, I pray you, to prevent virtue existing apart from pleasure? of course the reason is that all good things derive their origin from virtue, and therefore even those things which you cherish and seek for come originally from its roots. Yet, if they were entirely inseparable, we should not see some things to be pleasant, but not honourable, and others most honourable indeed, but hard and only to be attained by suffering. Add to this, that pleasure visits the basest lives, but virtue cannot co-exist with an evil life; yet some unhappy people are not without pleasure, nay, it is owing to pleasure itself that they are unhappy; and this could not take place if pleasure had any connexion with virtue, whereas virtue is often without pleasure, and never stands in need of it. Why do you put together two things which are unlike and even incompatible one with another? virtue is a lofty quality, sublime, royal, unconquerable, untiring: pleasure is low, slavish, weakly, perishable; its haunts and homes are the brothel and the tavern. You will meet virtue in the temple, the market-place, the senate house, manning the walls, covered with dust, sunburnt, horny-handed: you will find pleasure skulking out of sight, seeking for shady nooks at the public baths, hot chambers, and places which dread the visits of the aedile, soft, effeminate, reeking of wine and perfumes, pale or perhaps painted and made up with cosmetics. The highest good is immortal: it knows no ending, and does not admit of either satiety or regret: for a right-thinking mind never alters or becomes hateful to itself, nor do the best things ever undergo any change: but pleasure dies at the very moment when it charms us most: it has no great scope, and therefore it soon cloys and wearies us, and fades away as soon as its first impulse is over: indeed, we cannot depend upon anything whose nature is to change. Consequently it is not even possible that there should be any solid substance in that which comes and goes so swiftly, and which perishes by the very exercise of its own functions, for it arrives at a point at which it ceases to be, and even while it is beginning always keeps its end in view.

CHAPTER EIGHT

What answer are we to make to the reflexion that pleasure belongs to good and bad men alike, and that bad men take as much delight in their shame as good men in noble things? This was why the ancients bade us lead the highest, not the most pleasant life, in order that pleasure might not be the guide but the companion of a right-thinking and honourable mind; for it is Nature whom we ought to make our guide: let our reason watch her, and be advised by her. To live happily, then, is the same thing as to live according to Nature: what this may be, I will explain. If we guard the endowments of the body and the advantages of nature with care and fearlessness, as things soon to depart and given to us only for a day; if we do not fall under their dominion, nor allow ourselves to become the slaves of what is no part of our own being; if we assign to all bodily pleasures and external delights the same position which is held by auxiliaries and light-armed troops in a camp; if we make them our servants, not our masters—then and then only are they of value to our minds. A man should be unbiased and not to be conquered by external things: he ought to admire himself alone, to feel confidence in his own spirit, and so to order his life as to be ready alike for good or for bad fortune. Let not his confidence be without knowledge, nor his knowledge without steadfastness: let him always abide by what he has once determined, and let there be no erasure in his doctrines. It will be understood, even though I append it not, that such a man will be tranquil and composed in his demeanour, high-minded and courteous in his actions. Let reason be encouraged by the senses to seek for the truth, and draw its first principles from thence: indeed it has no other base of operations or place from which to start in pursuit of truth: it must fall back upon itself. Even the all-embracing universe and God who is its guide extends himself forth into outward things, and yet altogether returns from all sides back to himself. Let our mind do the same thing: when, following its bodily senses it has by means of them sent itself forth into the things of the outward world, let it remain still their master and its own. By this means we shall obtain a strength and an ability which are united and allied together, and shall derive from it that reason which never halts between two opinions, nor is dull in forming its perceptions, beliefs, or convictions. Such a mind, when it has ranged itself in order, made its various parts agree together, and, if I may so express myself, harmonized them, has attained to the highest good: for it has nothing evil or hazardous remaining, nothing to shake it or make it stumble: it will do everything under the guidance of its own will, and nothing unexpected will befall it, but whatever may be done by it will turn out well, and that, too, readily and easily, without the doer having recourse to any underhand devices: for slow and hesitating action are the signs of discord and want of settled purpose. You may, then, boldly declare that the highest good is singleness of mind: for where agreement and unity are, there must the virtues be: it is the vices that are at war one with another.

CHAPTER NINE

"But," says our adversary, "you yourself only practise virtue because you hope to obtain some pleasure from it." In the first place, even though virtue may afford us pleasure, still we do not seek after her on that account: for she does not bestow this, but bestows this to boot, nor is this the end for which she labours, but her labour wins this also, although it be directed to another end. As in a tilled-field, when ploughed for corn, some flowers are found amongst it, and yet, though these posies may charm the eye, all this labour was not spent in order to produce them — the man who sowed the field had another object in view, he gained this over and above it — so pleasure is not the reward or the cause of virtue, but comes in addition to it; nor do we choose virtue because she gives us pleasure, but she gives us pleasure also if we choose her. The highest good lies in the act of choosing her, and in the attitude of the noblest minds, which when once it has fulfilled its function and established itself within its own limits has attained to the highest good, and needs nothing more: for there is nothing outside of the whole, any more than there is anything beyond the end. You are mistaken, therefore, when you ask me what it is on account of which I seek after virtue: for you are seeking for something above the highest. Do you ask what I seek from virtue? I answer, Herself: for she has nothing better; she is her own reward. Does this not appear great enough, when I tell you that the highest good is an unyielding strength of mind, wisdom, magnanimity, sound judgment, freedom, harmony, beauty? Do you still ask me for something greater, of which these may be regarded as the attributes? Why do you talk of pleasures to me? I am seeking to find what is good for man, not for his belly; why, cattle and whales have larger ones than he.

CHAPTER TEN

"You purposely misunderstand what I say," says he, "for I too say that no one can live pleasantly unless he lives honorably also, and this cannot be the case with dumb animals who measure the extent of their happiness by that of their food. I loudly and publicly proclaim that what I call a pleasant life cannot exist without the addition of virtue." Yet who does not know that the greatest fools drink the deepest of those pleasures of yours? or that vice is full of enjoyments, and that the mind itself suggests to itself many perverted, vicious forms of pleasure ? — in the first place arrogance, excessive self-esteem, swaggering precedence over other men, a shortsighted, nay, a blind devotion to his own interests, dissolute luxury, excessive delight springing from the most trifling and childish causes, and also talkativeness, pride that takes a pleasure in insulting others, sloth, and the decay of a dull mind which goes to sleep over itself. All these are dissipated by virtue, which plucks a man by the ear, and measures the value of pleasures before she permits them to be used; nor does she set much store by those which she allows to pass current, for she merely allows their use, and her cheerfulness is not due to her use of them, but to her moderation in using them. "Yet when moderation lessens pleasure, it impairs the highest good." You devote yourself to pleasures, I check them; you indulge in pleasure, I use it; you think that it is the highest good, I do not even think it to be good: for the sake of pleasure I do nothing, you do everything.

CHAPTER ELEVEN

When I say that I do nothing for the sake of pleasure, I allude to that wise man, whom alone you admit to be capable of pleasure: now I do not call a man wise who is overcome by anything, let alone by pleasure: yet, if engrossed by pleasure, how will he resist toil, danger, want, and all the ills which surround and threaten the life of man? How will he bear the sight of death or of pain? How will he endure the tumult of the world, and make head against so many most active foes, if he be conquered by so effeminate an antagonist? He will do whatever pleasure advises him: well, do you not see how many things it will advise him to do ? "It will not," says our adversary, "be able to give him any bad advice, because it is combined with virtue?" Again, do you not see what a poor kind of highest good that must be which requires a guardian to ensure its being good at all? and how is virtue to rule pleasure if she follows it, seeing that to follow is the duty of a subordinate, to rule that of a commander? do you put that which commands in the background? According to your school, virtue has the dignified office of preliminary tester of pleasures. We shall, however, see whether virtue still remains virtue among those who treat her with such contempt, for if she leaves her proper station she can no longer keep her proper name: in the meanwhile, to keep to the point, I will show you many men beset by pleasures, men upon whom Fortune has showered all her gifts, whom you must needs admit to be bad men. Look at Nomentanus and Apicius, who digest all the good things, as they call them, of the sea and land, and review upon their tables the whole animal kingdom. Look at them as they lie on beds of roses gloating over their banquet, delighting their ears with music, their eyes with exhibitions, their palates with flavours: their whole bodies are titillated with soft and soothing applications, and lest even their nostrils should be idle, the very place in which they solemnized[1] the rites of luxury is scented with various perfumes. You will say that these men live in the midst of pleasures. Yet they are ill at ease, because they take pleasure in what is not good.

---

1. *Parentatur* seems to mean where an offering is made to luxury — where they sacrifice to luxury. Perfumes were used at funerals. Lipsius suggests that these feasts were like funerals because the guests were carried away from them dead drunk.

CHAPTER TWELVE

"They are ill at ease," replies he, " because many things arise which distract their thoughts, and their minds are disquieted by conflicting opinions." I admit that this is true: still these very men, foolish, inconsistent, and certain to feel remorse as they are, do nevertheless receive great pleasure, and we must allow that in so doing they are as far from feeling any trouble as they are from forming a right judgment, and that, as is the case with many people, they are possessed by a merry madness, and laugh while they rave. The pleasures of wise men, on the other hand, are mild, decorous, verging on dullness, kept under restraint and scarcely noticeable, and are neither invited to come nor received with honour when they come of their own accord, nor are they welcomed with any delight by those whom they visit, who mix them up with their lives and fill up empty spaces with them, like an amusing farce in the intervals of serious business. Let them no longer, then, join incongruous matters together, or connect pleasure with virtue, a mistake whereby they court the worst of men. The reckless profligate, always in liquor and belching out the fumes of wine, believes that he lives with virtue, because he knows that he lives with pleasure, for he hears it said that pleasure cannot exist apart from virtue; consequently he dubs his vices with the title of wisdom and parades all that he ought to conceal. So, men are not encouraged by Epicurus to run riot, but the vicious hide their excesses in the lap of philosophy, and flock to the schools in which they hear the praises of pleasure. They do not consider how sober and temperate — for so, by Hercules, I believe it to be — that " pleasure " of Epicurus is, but they rush at his mere name, seeking to obtain some protection and cloak for their vices. They lose, therefore, the one virtue which their evil life possessed, that of being ashamed of doing wrong: for they praise what they used to blush at, and boast of their vices. Thus modesty can never reassert itself, when shameful idleness is dignified with an honourable name. The reason why that praise which your school lavishes upon pleasure is so hurtful, is because the honourable part of its teaching passes unnoticed, but the degrading part is seen by all.

CHAPTER THIRTEEN

I myself believe, though my Stoic comrades would be unwilling to hear me say so, that the teaching of Epicurus was upright and holy, and even, if you examine it narrowly, stern: for this much talked of pleasure is reduced to a very narrow compass, and he bids pleasure submit to the same law which we bid virtue do — I mean, to obey nature. Luxury, however, is not satisfied with what is enough for nature. What is the consequence? Whoever thinks that happiness consists in lazy sloth, and alternations of gluttony and profligacy, requires a good patron for a bad action, and when he has become an Epicurean, having been led to do so by the attractive name of that school, he follows, not the pleasure which he there hears spoken of, but that which he brought thither with him, and, having learned to think that his vices coincide with the maxims of that philosophy, he indulges in them no longer timidly and in dark corners, but boldly in the face of day. I will not, therefore, like most of our school, say that the sect of Epicurus is the teacher of crime, but what I say is: it is ill spoken of, it has a bad reputation, and yet it does not deserve it. "Who can know this without having been admitted to its inner mysteries?" Its very outside gives opportunity for scandal, and encourages men's baser desires: it is like a brave man dressed in a woman's gown: your chastity is assured, your manhood is safe, your body is submitted to nothing disgraceful, but your hand holds a drum (like a priest of Cybele). Choose, then, some honourable superscription for your school, some writing which shall in itself arouse the mind: that which at present stands over your door has been invented by the vices. He who ranges himself on the side of virtue gives thereby a proof of a noble disposition : he who follows pleasure appears to be weakly, worn out, degrading his manhood, likely to fall into infamous vices unless someone discriminates his pleasures for him, so that he may know which remain within the bounds of natural desire, which are frantic and boundless, and become all the more insatiable the more they are satisfied. But come! let virtue lead the way: then every step will be safe. Too much pleasure is hurtful: but with virtue we need fear no excess of any kind, because moderation is contained in virtue herself. That which is injured by its own extent cannot be a good thing: besides, what better guide can there be than reason for beings endowed with a reasoning nature? so if this combination pleases you, if you are willing to proceed to a happy life thus accompanied, let virtue lead the way, let pleasure follow and hang about the body like a shadow: it is the part of a mind incapable of great things to hand over virtue, the highest of all qualities, as a handmaid to pleasure.

CHAPTER FOURTEEN

Let virtue lead the way and bear the standard: we shall have pleasure for all that, but we shall be her masters and controllers; she may win some concessions from us, but will not force us to do anything. On the contrary, those who have permitted pleasure to lead the van, have neither one nor the other: for they lose virtue altogether, and yet they do not possess pleasure, but are possessed by it, and are either tortured by its absence or choked by its excess, being wretched if deserted by it, and yet more wretched if overwhelmed by it, like those who are caught in the shoals of the Syrtes and at one time are left on dry ground and at another tossed on the flowing waves. This arises from an exaggerated want of self-control, and a hidden love of evil: for it is dangerous for one who seeks after evil instead of good to attain his object. As we hunt wild beasts with toil and peril, and even when they are caught find them an anxious possession, for they often tear their keepers to pieces, even so are great pleasures: they turn out to be great evils and take their owners prisoner. The more numerous and the greater they are, the more inferior and the slave of more masters does that man become whom the vulgar call a happy man. I may even press this analogy further: as the man who tracks wild animals to their lairs, and who sets great store on — "Seeking with snares the wandering brutes to noose," and "Making their hounds the spacious glade surround," that he may follow their tracks, neglects far more desirable things, and leaves many duties unfulfilled, so he who pursues pleasure postpones everything to it, disregards that first essential, liberty, and sacrifices it to his belly; nor does he buy pleasure for himself, but sells himself to pleasure.

CHAPTER FIFTEEN

"But what," asks our adversary, "is there to hinder virtue and pleasure being combined together, and a highest good being thus formed, so that honour and pleasure may be the same thing?" Because nothing except what is honourable can form a part of honour, and the highest good would lose its purity if it were to see within itself anything unlike its own better part. Even the joy which arises from virtue, although it be a good thing, yet is not a part of absolute good, any more than cheerfulness or peace of mind, which are indeed good things, but which merely follow the highest good, and do not contribute to its perfection, although they are generated by the noblest causes. Whoever on the other hand forms an alliance, and that, too, a one-sided one, between virtue and pleasure, clogs whatever strength the one may possess by the weakness of the other, and sends liberty under the yoke, for liberty can only remain unconquered as long as she knows nothing more valuable than herself: for he begins to need the help of Fortune, which is the most utter slavery: his life becomes anxious, full of suspicion, timorous, fearful of accidents, waiting in agony for critical moments of time. You do not afford virtue a solid immoveable base if you bid it stand on what is unsteady: and what can be so unsteady as dependence on mere chance, and the vicissitudes of the body and of those things which act on the body? How can such a man obey God and receive everything which comes to pass in a cheerful spirit, never complaining of fate, and putting a good construction upon everything that befalls him, if he be agitated by the petty pin-pricks of pleasures and pains? A man cannot be a good protector of his country, a good avenger of her wrongs, or a good defender of his friends, if he be inclined to pleasures. Let the highest good, then, rise to that height from whence no force can dislodge it, whither neither pain can ascend, nor hope, nor fear, nor anything else that can impair the authority of the " highest good." Thither virtue alone can make her way: by her aid that hill must be climbed: she will bravely stand her ground and endure whatever may befall her not only resignedly, but even willingly: she will know that all hard times come in obedience to natural laws, and like a good soldier she will bear wounds, count scars, and when transfixed and dying will yet adore the general for whom she falls: she will bear in mind the old maxim " Follow God." On the other hand, he who grumbles and complains and bemoans himself is nevertheless forcibly obliged to obey orders, and is dragged away, however much against his will, to carry them out: yet what madness is it to be dragged rather than to follow? as great, by Hercules, as it is folly and ignorance of one's true position to grieve because one has not got something or because something has caused us rough treatment, or to be surprised or indignant at those ills which befall good men as well as bad ones, I mean diseases, deaths, illnesses, and the other cross accidents of human life. Let us bear with magnanimity whatever the system of the universe makes it needful for us to bear: we are all bound by this oath: "To bear the ills of mortal life, and to submit with a good grace to what we cannot avoid." We have been born into a monarchy: our liberty is to obey God.

CHAPTER SIXTEEN

True happiness, therefore, consists in virtue: and what will this virtue bid you do? Not to think anything bad or good which is connected neither with virtue nor with wickedness: and in the next place, both to endure un moved the assaults of evil, and, as far as is right, to form a god out of what is good. What reward does she promise you for this campaign? an enormous one, and one that raises you to the level of the gods: you shall be subject to no restraint and to no want; you shall be free, safe, unhurt; you shall fail in nothing that you attempt; you shall be debarred from nothing; everything shall turn out according to your wish; no misfortune shall befall you; nothing shall happen to you except what you expect and hope for. "What! does virtue alone suffice to make you happy?" why, of course, consummate and god-like virtue such as this not only suffices, but more than suffices: for when a man is placed beyond the reach of any desire, what can he possibly lack? if all that he needs is concentred in himself, how can he require anything from without? He, however, who is only on the road to virtue, although he may have made great progress along it, nevertheless needs some favour from fortune while he is still struggling among mere human interests, while he is untying that knot, and all the bonds which bind him to mortality. What, then, is the difference between them? it is that some are tied more or less tightly by these bonds, and some have even tied themselves with them as well; whereas he who has made progress towards the upper regions and raised himself upwards drags a looser chain, and though not yet free, is yet as good as free.

CHAPTER SEVENTEEN

If, therefore, any one of those dogs who yelp at philosophy were to say, as they are wont to do, "Why, then, do you talk so much more bravely than you live? why do you check your words in the presence of your superiors, and consider money to be a necessary implement:' why are you disturbed when you sustain losses, and weep on hearing of the death of your wife or your friend? Why do you pay regard to common rumour, and feel annoyed by calumnious gossip? why is your estate more elaborately kept than its natural use requires? why do you not dine according to your own maxims? why is your furniture smarter than it need be? why do you drink wine that is older than yourself? why are your grounds laid out? Why do you plant trees which afford nothing except shade? why does your wife wear in her ears the price of a rich man's house? why are your children at school dressed in costly clothes? why is it a science to wait upon you at table? why is your silver plate not set down anyhow or at random, but skillfully disposed in regular order, with a superintendent to preside over the carving of the viands?" Add to this, if you like, the questions "Why do you own property beyond the seas? why do you own more than you know of? it is a shame to you not to know your slaves by sight: for you must be very neglectful of them if you only own a few, or very extravagant if you have too many for your memory to retain." I will add some reproaches afterwards, and will bring more accusations against myself than you think of: for the present I will make you the following answer. "I am not a wise man, and I will not be one in order to feed your spite: so do not require me to be on a level with the best of men, but merely to be better than the worst: I am satisfied, if every day I take away something from my vices and correct my faults. I have not arrived at perfect soundness of mind, indeed, I never shall arrive at it: I compound palliatives rather than remedies for my gout, and am satisfied if it comes at rarer interval - and does not shoot so painfully. Compared with your feet, which are lame, I am a racer." I make this speech, not on my own behalf, for I am steeped in vices of every kind, but on behalf of one who has made some progress in virtue.

CHAPTER EIGHTEEN

"You talk one way," objects our adversary, "and live another." You most spiteful of creatures, you who always show the bitterest hatred to the best of men, this reproach was flung at Plato, at Epicurus, at Zeno: for all these declared how they ought to live, not how they did live. I speak of virtue, not of myself, and when I blame vices, I blame my own first of all: when I have the power, I shall live as I ought to do: spite, however deeply steeped in venom, shall not keep me back from what is best: that poison itself with which you bespatter others, with which you choke yourselves, shall not hinder me from continuing to praise that life which I do not, indeed, lead, but which I know I ought to lead, from loving virtue and from following after her, albeit a long way behind her and with halting gait. Am I to expect that evil speaking will respect anything, seeing that it respected neither Rutilius nor Cato? Will anyone care about being thought too rich by men for whom Diogenes the Cynic was not poor enough? That most energetic philosopher fought against all the desires of the body, and was poorer even than the other Cynics, in that besides having given up possessing anything he had also given up asking for anything: yet they reproached him for not being sufficiently in want: as though forsooth it were poverty, not virtue, of which he professed knowledge.

CHAPTER NINETEEN

They say that Diodorus, the Epicurean philosopher, who within these last few days put an end to his life with his own hand, did not act according to the precepts of Epicurus, in cutting his throat: some choose to regard this act as the result of madness, others of recklessness; he, meanwhile, happy and filled with the consciousness of his own goodness, has borne testimony to himself by his manner of departing from life, has commended the repose of a life spent at anchor in a safe harbour, and has said what you do not like to hear, because you too ought to do it.

"I've lived, I've run the race which Fortune set me."

You argue about the life and death of another, and yelp at the name of men whom some peculiarly noble quality has rendered great, just as tiny curs do at the approach of strangers: for it is to your interest that no one should appear to be good, as if virtue in another were a reproach to all your crimes. You enviously compare the glories of others with your own dirty actions, and do not understand how greatly to your disadvantage it is to venture to do so: for if they who follow after virtue be greedy, lustful, and fond of power, what must you be, who hate the very name of virtue? You say that no one acts up to his professions, or lives according to the standard which he sets up in his discourses: what wonder, seeing that the words which they speak are brave, gigantic, and able to weather all the storms which wreck mankind, whereas they themselves are struggling to tear themselves away from crosses into which each one of you is driving his own nail. Yet men who are crucified hang from one single pole, but these who punish themselves are divided between as many crosses as they have lusts, but yet are given to evil speaking, and are so magnificent in their contempt of the vices of others that I should suppose that they had none of their own, were it not that some criminals when on the gibbet spit upon the spectators.

CHAPTER TWENTY

"Philosophers do not carry into effect all that they teach." No; but they effect much good by their teaching, by the noble thoughts which they conceive in their minds: would, indeed, that they could act up to their talk: what could be happier than they would be? but in the meanwhile you have no right to despise good sayings and hearts full of good thoughts. Men deserve praise for engaging in profitable studies, even though they stop short of producing any results. Why need we wonder if those who begin to climb a steep path do not succeed in ascending it very high? yet, if you be a man, look with respect on those who attempt great things, even though they fall. It is the act of a generous spirit to proportion its efforts not to its own strength but to that of human nature, to entertain lofty aims, and to conceive plans which are too vast to be carried into execution even by those who are endowed with gigantic intellects, who appoint for themselves the following rules: "I will look upon death or upon a comedy with the same expression of countenance : I will submit to labours, however great they may be, supporting the strength of my body by that of my mind: I will despise riches when I have them as much as when I have them not; if they be elsewhere I will not be more gloomy, if they sparkle around me I will not be more lively than I should otherwise be: whether Fortune comes or goes I will take no notice of her: I will view all lands as though they belong to me, and my own as though they belonged to all mankind: I will so live as to remember that I was born for others, and will thank Nature on this account: for in what fashion could she have done better for me? she has given me alone to all, and all to me alone. Whatever I may possess, I will neither hoard it greedily nor squander it recklessly. I will think that I have no possessions so real as those which I have given away to deserving people: I will not reckon benefits by their magnitude or number, or by anything except the value set upon them by the receiver: I never will consider a gift to be a large one if it be bestowed upon a worthy object. I will do nothing because of public opinion, but everything because of conscience: whenever I do anything alone by myself I will believe that the eyes of the Roman people are upon me while I do it. In eating and drinking my object shall be to quench the desires of Nature, not to fill and empty my belly. I will be agreeable with my friends, gentle and mild to my foes: I will grant pardon before I am asked for it, and will meet the wishes of honourable men half way: I will bear in mind that the world is my native city, that its governors are the gods, and that they stand above and around me, criticizing whatever I do or say. Whenever either Nature demands my breath again, or reason bids me dismiss it, I will quit this life, calling all to witness that I have loved a good conscience, and good pursuits; that no one's freedom, my own least of all, has been impaired through me." He who sets up these as the rules of his life will soar aloft and strive to make his way to the gods: of a truth, even though he fails, yet he

"Fails in a high emprise."[1]

But you, who hate both virtue and those who practise it, do nothing at which we need be surprised, for sickly lights cannot bear the sun, nocturnal creatures avoid the brightness of day, and at its first dawning become bewildered and all betake themselves to their dens together: creatures that fear the light hide themselves in crevices. So croak away, and exercise your miserable tongues in reproaching good men : open wide your jaws, bite hard: you will break many teeth before you make any impression.

---

1. The quotation is from the epitaph on Phaeton.—See Ovid, Met. II. 327.

CHAPTER TWENTY-ONE

"But how is it that this man studies philosophy and nevertheless lives the life of a rich man? Why does he say that wealth ought to be despised and yet possess it? that life should be despised, and yet live? that health should be despised, and yet guard it with the utmost care, and wish it to be as good as possible? Does he consider banishment to be an empty name, and say, "What evil is there in changing one country for another?" and yet, if permitted, does he not grow old in his native land? does he declare that there is no difference between a longer and a shorter time, and yet, if he be not prevented, lengthen out his life and flourish in a green old age?" His answer is, that these things ought to be despised, not that he should not possess them, but that he should not possess them with fear and trembling: he does not drive them away from him, but when they leave him he follows after them unconcernedly. Where, indeed, can fortune invest riches more securely than in a place from whence they can always be recovered without any squabble with their trustee? Marcus Cato, when he was praising Curius and Coruncanius and that century in which the possession of a few small silver coins were an offence which was punished by the Censor, himself owned four million sesterces; a less fortune, no doubt, than that of Crassus, but larger than of Cato the Censor. If the amounts be compared, he had outstripped his great-grandfather further than he himself was outdone by Crassus, and if still greater riches had fallen to his lot, he would not have spurned them: for the wise man does not think himself unworthy of any chance presents: he does not love riches, but he prefers to have them; he does not receive them into his spirit, but only into his house: nor does he cast away from him what he already possesses, but keeps them, and is willing that his virtue should receive a larger subject-matter for its exercise.

CHAPTER TWENTY-TWO

Who can doubt, however, that the wise man, if he is rich, has a wider field for the development of his powers than if he is poor, seeing that in the latter case the only virtue which he can display is that of neither being perverted nor crushed by his poverty, whereas if he has riches, he will have a wide field for the exhibition of temperance, generosity, laboriousness, methodical arrangement, and grandeur. The wise man will not despise himself, however short of stature he may be, but nevertheless he will wish to be tall: even though he be feeble and one-eyed he may be in good health, yet he would prefer to have bodily strength, and that too, while he knows all the while that he has something which is even more powerful: he will endure illness, and will hope for good health: for some things, though they may be trifles compared with the sum total, and though they may be taken away without destroying the chief good, yet add somewhat to that constant cheerfulness which arises from virtue. Riches encourage and brighten up such a man just as a sailor is delighted at a favourable wind that bears him on his way, or as people feel pleasure at a fine day or at a sunny spot in the cold weather. What wise man, I mean of our school, whose only good is virtue, can deny that even these matters which we call neither good nor bad have in themselves a certain value, and that some of them are preferable to others? to some of them we show a certain amount of respect, and to some a great deal. Do not, then, make any mistake: riches belong to the class of desirable things. "Why then," say you, "do you laugh at me, since you place them in the same position that I do?" Do you wish to know how different the position is in which we place them? If my riches leave me, they will carry away with them nothing except themselves: you will be bewildered and will seem to be left without yourself if they should pass away from you: with me riches occupy a certain place, but with you they occupy the highest place of all. In fine, my riches belong to me, you belong to your riches.

CHAPTER TWENTY-THREE

Cease, then, forbidding philosophers to possess money: no one has condemned wisdom to poverty. The philosopher may own ample wealth, but will not own wealth that which has been torn from another, or which is stained with another's blood: his must be obtained without wronging any man, and without its being won by base means; it must be alike honourably come by and honourably spent, and must be such as spite alone could shake its head at. Raise it to whatever figure you please, it will still be an honourable possession, if, while it includes much which every man would like to call his own, there be nothing which any one can say is his own. Such a man will not forfeit his right to the favour of Fortune, and will neither boast of his inheritance nor blush for it if it was honourably acquired: yet he will have something to boast of, if he throw his house open, let all his countrymen come among his property, and say, "If any one recognizes here anything belonging to him, let him take it." What a great man, how excellently rich will he be, if after this speech he possesses as much as he had before! I say, then, that if he can safely and confidently submit his accounts to the scrutiny of the people, and no one can find in them any item upon which he can lay hands, such a man may boldly and unconcealedly enjoy his riches. The wise man will not allow a single ill-won penny to cross his threshold: yet he will not refuse or close his door against great riches, if they are the gift of fortune and the product of virtue: what reason has he for grudging them good quarters: let them come and be his guests: he will neither brag of them nor hide them away: the one is the part of a silly, the other of a cowardly and paltry spirit, which, as it were, muffles up a good thing in its lap. Neither will he, as I said before, turn them out of his house: for what will he say? will he say, " You are useless," or " I do not know how to use riches?" As he is capable of performing a journey upon his own feet, but yet would prefer to mount a carriage, just so he will be capable of being poor, yet will wish to be rich; he will own wealth, but will view it as an uncertain possession which will someday fly away from him. He will not allow it to be a burden either to himself or to any one else: he will give it — why do you prick up your ears? why do you open your pockets?—he will give it either to good men or to those whom it may make into good men. He will give it after having taken the utmost pains to choose those who are fittest to receive it, as becomes one who bears in mind that he ought to give an account of what he spends as well as of what he receives. He will give for good and commendable reasons, for a gift ill bestowed counts as a shameful loss: he will have an easily opened pocket, but not one with a hole in it, so that much may be taken out of it, yet nothing may fall out of it.

CHAPTER TWENTY-FOUR

He who believes giving to be an easy matter, is mistaken: it offers very great difficulties, if we bestow our bounty rationally, and do not scatter it impulsively and at random. I do this man a service, I requite a good turn done me by that one: I help this other, because I pity him: this man, again, I teach to be no fit object for poverty to hold down or degrade. I shall not give some men anything, although they are in want, because, even if I do give to them they will still be in want: I shall proffer my bounty to some, and shall forcibly thrust it upon others: I cannot be neglecting my own interests while I am doing this: at no time do I make more people in my debt than when I am giving things away. "What ?" say you, " do you give that you. may receive again?" At any rate I do not give that I may throw my bounty away: what I give should be so placed that although I cannot ask for its return, yet it may be given back to me. A benefit should be invested in the same manner as a treasure buried deep in the earth, which you would not dig up unless actually obliged. Why, what opportunities of conferring benefits the mere house of a rich man affords? for who considers generous behaviour due only to those who wear the toga? Nature bids me do good to mankind—what difference does it make whether they be slaves or freemen, free-born or emancipated, whether their freedom be legally acquired or bestowed by arrangement among friends? Wherever there is a human being, there is an opportunity for a benefit: consequently, money may be distributed even within one's own threshold, and a field may be found there for the practice of freehandedness, which is not so called because it is our duty towards free men, but because it takes its rise in a free-born mind. In the case of the wise man, this never falls upon base and unworthy recipients, and never becomes so exhausted as not, whenever it finds a worthy object, to flow as if its store was undiminished. You have, therefore, no grounds for misunderstanding the honourable, brave, and spirited language which you hear from those who are studying wisdom : and first of all observe this, that a student of wisdom is not the same thing as a man who has made himself perfect in wisdom. The former will say to you, "In my talk I express the most admirable sentiments, yet I am still weltering amid countless ills. You must not force me to act up to my rules: at the present time I am forming myself, moulding my character, and striving to rise myself to the height of a great example. If I should ever succeed in carrying out all that I have set myself to accomplish, you may then demand that my words and deeds should correspond." But he who has reached the summit of human perfection will deal otherwise with you, and will say, " In the first place, you have no business to allow yourself to sit in judgment upon your betters:" I have already obtained one proof of my righteousness in having become an object of dislike to bad men: however, to make you a rational answer, which I grudge to no man, listen to what I declare, and at what price I value all things. Riches, I say, are not a good thing; for if they were, they would make men good: now since that which is found even among bad men cannot be termed good, I do not allow them to be called so: nevertheless I admit that they are desirable and useful and contribute great comforts to our lives.

CHAPTER TWENTY-FIVE

Learn, then, since we both agree that they are desirable, what my reason is amongst counting them among good things, and in what respects I should behave differently to you if I possessed them. Place me as master in the house of a very rich man: place me where gold and silver plate is used for the commonest purposes; I shall not think more of myself because of things which even though they are in my house are yet no part of me. Take me away to the wooden bridge[1] and put me down there among the beggars: I shall not despise myself because I am sitting among those who hold out their hands for alms: for what can the lack of a piece of bread matter to one who does not lack the power of dying? Well, then? I prefer the magnificent house to the beggar's bridge. Place me among magnificent furniture and all the appliances of luxury: I shall not think myself any happier because my, cloak is soft, because my guests rest upon purple.

Change the scene: I shall be no more miserable if my weary head rests upon a bundle of hay, if I lie upon a cushion from the circus, with all the stuffing on the point of coming out through its patches of threadbare cloth. Well, then? I prefer, as far as my feelings go, to show myself in public dressed in woollen and in robes of office, rather than with naked or half-covered shoulders: I should like every day's business to turn out just as I wish it to do, and new congratulations to be constantly following upon the former ones: yet I will not pride myself upon this: change all this good fortune for its opposite, let my spirit be distracted by losses, grief, various kinds of attacks: let no hour pass without some dispute: I shall not on this account, though beset by the greatest miseries, call myself the most miserable of beings, nor shall I curse any particular day, for I have taken care to have no unlucky days. What, then, is the upshot of all this? it is that I prefer to have to regulate joys than to stifle sorrows. The great Socrates would say the same thing to you. "Make me," he would say, "the conqueror of all nations: let the voluptuous car of Bacchus bear me in triumph to Thebes from the rising of the sun: let the kings of the Persians receive laws from me: yet I shall feel myself to be a man at the very moment when all around salute me as a God. Straightway connect this lofty height with a headlong fall into misfortune: let me be placed upon a foreign chariot that I may grace the triumph of a proud and savage conqueror: I will follow another's car with no more humility than I showed when I stood in my own. What then? In spite of all this, I had rather be a conqueror than a captive. I despise the whole dominion of Fortune, but still, if I were given my choice, I would choose its better parts. I shall make whatever befalls me become a good thing, but I prefer that what befalls me should be comfortable and pleasant and unlikely to cause me annoyance: for you need not suppose that any virtue exists without labour, but some virtues need spurs, while others need the curb. As we have to check our body on a downward path, and to urge it to climb a steep one; so also the path of some virtues leads downhill, that of others uphill. Can we doubt that patience, courage, constancy, and all the other virtues which have to meet strong opposition, and to trample Fortune under their feet, are climbing, struggling, winning their way up a steep ascent? Why! is it not equally evident that generosity, moderation, and gentleness glide easily downhill? With the latter we must hold in our spirit, lest it run away with us: with the former we must urge and spur it on. We ought, therefore to apply these energetic, combative virtues to poverty, and to riches those other more thrifty ones which trip lightly along, and merely support their own weight. This being the distinction between them, I would rather have to deal with those which I could practise in comparative quiet, than those of which one can only make trial through blood and sweat. "Wherefore," says the sage, " I do not talk one way and live another: but you do not rightly understand what I say: the sound of my words alone reaches your ears, you do not try to find out their meaning."

1. The " Pons Sublicius," or "pile bridge," was built over the Tiber by Aliens Martins, one of the early kings of Rome, and was always kept in repair out of a superstitious feeling.

CHAPTER TWENTY-SIX

"What difference, then, is there between me, who am a fool, and you, who are a wise man?" "All the difference in the world: for riches are slaves in the house of a wise man, but masters in that of a fool. You accustom yourself to them and cling to them as if somebody had promised that they should be yours forever, but a wise man never thinks so much about poverty as when he is surrounded by riches. No general ever trusts so implicitly is the maintenance of peace as not to make himself ready for a war, which, though it may not actually be waged, has nevertheless been declared; you are rendered over-proud by a fine house, as though it could never be burned or fall down, and your heads are turned by riches as though they were beyond the reach of all dangers and were so great that Fortune has not sufficient strength to swallow them up. You sit idly playing with your wealth and do not foresee the perils in store for it, as savages generally do when besieged, for, not understanding the use of siege artillery, they look on idly at the labours of the besiegers and do not understand the object of the machines which they are putting together at a distance: and this is exactly what happens to you: you go to sleep over your property, and never reflect how many misfortunes loom menacingly around you on all sides, and soon will plunder you of costly spoils , but if one takes away riches from the wise man, one leaves him still in possession of all that is his: for he lives happy in the present, and without fear for the future. The great Socrates, or anyone else who had the same superiority to and power to withstand the things of this life, would say,' I have no more fixed principle than that of not altering the course of my life to suit your prejudices: you may pour your accustomed talk upon me from all sides: I shall not think that you are abusing me, but that you are merely wailing like poor little babies.'" This is what the man will say who possesses wisdom, whose mind, being free from, vices, bids him reproach others, not because he hates them, but in order to improve them: and to this he will add, "Your opinion of me affects me with pain, not for my own sake but for yours, because to hate perfection and to assail virtue is in itself a resignation of all hope of doing well. You do me no harm; neither do men harm the gods when they overthrow their altars: but it is clear that your intention is an evil one and that you will wish to do -harm even where you are not able. I bear with your prating in the same spirit in which Jupiter, best and greatest, bears with the idle tales of the poets, one of whom represents him with wings, another with horns, another as an adulterer staying out all night, another is dealing harshly with the gods, another as unjust to men, another as the seducer of noble youths whom he carries off by force, and those, too, his own relatives, another as a parricide and the conqueror of another's kingdom, and that his father's. The only result of such tales is that men feel less shame at committing sin if they believe the gods to be guilty of such actions. But although this conduct of yours does not hurt me, yet, for your own sakes, I advise you, respect virtue: believe those who having long followed her cry aloud that what they follow is a thing of might, and daily appears mightier. Reverence her as you would the gods, and reverence her followers as you would the priests of the gods: and whenever any mention of sacred writings is made, favete liyiguis, favour us with silence: this word is not derived, as most people imagine, from favour, but commands silence, that divine service may be performed without being interrupted by any words of evil omen. It is much more necessary that you should be ordered to do this, in order that whenever utterance is made by that oracle, you may listen to it with attention and in silence. Whenever anyone beats a sistrum[1], pretending to do so by divine command, any proficient in grazing his own skin covers his arms and shoulders with blood from light cuts, any one crawls on his knees howling along the street, or any old man clad in linen comes forth in daylight with a lamp and laurel branch and cries out that one of the gods is angry, you crowd round him and listen to his words, and each increases the other's wonderment by declaring him to be divinely inspired.

---

1. Sistrum. A metallic rattle used by the Egyptians in celebrating the rites of Isis, Sec.—Andrews.

CHAPTER TWENTY-SEVEN

Behold! from that prison of his, which by entering he cleansed from shame and rendered more honourable than any senate house, Socrates addresses you, saying: "What is this madness of yours? what is this disposition, at war alike with gods and men, which leads you to calumniate virtue and to outrage holiness with malicious accusations? Praise good men, if you are able: if not, pass them by in silence: if indeed you take pleasure in this offensive abusiveness, fall foul of one another: for when you rave against Heaven, I do not say that you commit sacrilege, but you waste your time. I once afforded Aristophanes with the subject of a jest: since then all the crew of comic poets have made me a mark for their envenomed wit: my virtue has been made to shine more brightly by the very blows which have been aimed at it, for it is to its advantage to be brought before the public and exposed to temptation, nor do any people understand its greatness more than those who by their assaults have made trial of its strength. The hardness of flint is known to none so well as to those who strike it. I offer myself to all attacks, like some lonely rock in a shallow sea, which the waves never cease to beat upon from whatever quarter they may come, but which they cannot thereby move from its place nor yet wear away, for however many years they may unceasingly dash against it. Bound upon me, rush upon me, I will overcome you by enduring your onset: whatever strikes against that which is firm and unconquerable merely injures itself by its own violence. Wherefore, seek some soft and yielding object to pierce with your darts. But have you leisure to peer into other men's evil deeds and to sit in judgment upon anybody? to ask how it is that this philosopher has so roomy a house, or that one so good a dinner? Do you look at other people's pimples while yon yourselves are covered with countless ulcers? This is as though one who was eaten up by the mange were to point with scorn at the moles and warts on the bodies of the handsomest men. Reproach Plato with having sought for money, reproach Aristotle with having obtained it, Democritus with having disregarded it, Epicurus with having spent it: cast Phaedrus and Alcibiades in my own teeth, you who reach the height of enjoyment whenever you get an opportunity of imitating our vices! Why do you not rather cast your eyes around yourselves at the ills which tear you to pieces on every side, some attacking you from without, some burning in your own bosoms? However little you know your own place, mankind has not yet come to such a pass that you can have leisure to wag your tongues to the reproach of your betters.

CHAPTER TWENTY-EIGHT

This you do not understand, and you bear a countenance which does not befit your condition, like many men who sit in the circus or the theatre without having learned that their home is already in mourning: but I, looking forward from a lofty standpoint, can see what storms are either threatening you, and will burst in torrents upon you somewhat later, or are close upon you and on the point of sweeping away all that you possess. Why, though you are hardly aware of it, is there not a whirling hurricane at this moment spinning round and confusing your minds, making them seek and avoid the very same things, now raising them aloft and now dashing them below?"

CONTENTS

Preface   1
Chapter 1   3
Chapter 2   6
Chapter 3   9
Chapter 4   12
Chapter 5   15
Chapter 6   17
Chapter 7   19
Chapter 8   21
Chapter 9   24
Chapter 10   26
Chapter 11   28
Chapter 12   30
Chapter 13   32
Chapter 14   35
Chapter 15   37
Chapter 16   40
Chapter 17   42
Chapter 18   44
Chapter 19   46
Chapter 20   48
Chapter 21   51
Chapter 22   53
Chapter 23   55
Chapter 24   58
Chapter 25   61
Chapter 26   65
Chapter 27   69
Chapter 28   72

Copyright © 2020 by FV Éditions
Translator : Aubrey Stewart
Hardcover ISBN : 979-10-299-0924-5
All Rights Reserved

www.ingramcontent.com/pod-product-compliance
Lightning Source LLC
LaVergne TN
LVHW091545070526
838199LV00002B/220